FEDERAL - HOCKING
SCHOOL DISTRICT

D1273868

JOHANNIS HEVELII
COMETOGRAPHIA.

The frontispiece of Hevelius's book Cometographia *shows three scientists arguing different theories about comets' paths.*

EARTH, SEA, AND SKY
THE WORK OF EDMOND HALLEY

LINDA WALVOORD GIRARD
ILLUSTRATED BY JAMES WATLING

ALBERT WHITMAN & COMPANY
NILES, ILLINOIS

For my father,
Christian Walvoord (1912–1985),
who missed Halley's Comet but showed me discovery.

Library of Congress Cataloging in Publication Data

Girard, Linda Walvoord.
   Earth, sea, and sky.

   Summary: Describes the life and varied scientific
work of the first man to track a comet's path and
accurately predict its return.
   1. Halley, Edmond, 1656-1742—Juvenile literature.
2. Comets—Juvenile literature. 3. Astronomers—
Great Britain—Biography—Juvenile literature.
[1. Halley, Edmond, 1656-1742. 2. Astronomers.
3. Comets] I. Watling, James, ill. II. Title.
QB36.H25G57 1985 520'.92'4 [B] [92] 85-15506
ISBN 0-8075-1868-9

The text of this book is printed in twelve-point Palatino

Text © 1985 by Linda Walvoord Girard
Illustrations © 1985 by James Watling
Published in 1985 by Albert Whitman & Company, Niles, Illinois
Published simultaneously in Canada by General Publishing, Limited, Toronto
Printed in U.S.A. All rights reserved.
10 9 8 7 6 5 4 3 2 1

CONTENTS

CHAPTER 1
THE GREAT COMET

ONE DARK, clear night in August 1682, in a house on the northern edge of London, a young man named Edmond Halley was peering at the sky through his telescope, as he often did on clear nights. The stars in their certain patterns beamed bright over the rolling land of England.

On this particular night, there among the stars he knew so well, Halley saw something different. It was blurry, like snow crystals on a glass with the sun behind them. The strange body had a bright head like a brilliant star and trailed streaks of light like hair.

Halley knew it wasn't a moon or a star. It wasn't a planet.

For an hour or more, he watched the light among the stars. He began to jot down notes as he eased the telescope back and forth. Though it moved slowly, this new light had suddenly appeared in his lens tonight as if out of nowhere.

"It's a comet, then," he said to himself, though not a soul was in the room to hear him.

Although he was only twenty-five years old, Edmond Halley was already regarded as a good astronomer. Four years before, he had been elected the youngest member, or fellow, of the Royal Society, an important club of the most honored scientists in England.

Each Thursday at three o'clock, the Royal Society met in fine, quiet rooms at Gresham College in London. There the members did experiments, discussed scientific news, and read papers telling of their discoveries. Sir Christopher Wren, the famous architect, was often there. He, too, was an astronomer, and he was president of the group that year. Robert Hooke, a brilliant professor of geometry, was also a member. (No women belonged to the Royal Society. In the 1600s, science was a man's world.)

When Halley told the members he was taking notes on the new comet, no one would have been surprised. The full name of the society was the Royal Society of London for Improving Natural Knowledge. Royal Society members were always busy observing and measuring many things in nature: the length of a fly's wing, the flow of water, the speed of a bird in flight. Someone had once told King Charles II of England that the Royal Society had weighed the air. The king thought that was a wonderful joke. But the Royal Society *had* weighed the air! To the society, Halley's plan to observe the comet would have seemed routine. He wasn't the first to see it.

Besides, no one thought Halley could follow the comet for long. Like all other comets, this one would disappear from the sky in a few weeks or months. That would be the end of Halley's measurements.

Through August and into September, Halley plotted the comet's positions as it moved across the sky. For each observation, he wrote down the date, the time, and the comet's exact location among the various stars. Because of the earth's motion, the stars seem to move throughout the night and throughout the seasons. By Halley's time, astronomers had watched these regular changes for centuries. Huge books that weighed many pounds could be hauled down off shelves to tell an astronomer where each star would appear at any given time. Once a comet was plotted against the stars, any future astronomer could figure out exactly where in the sky it had been.

Halley plotted.

Night after night, he made notes. He saved them all. We still have the notebook he used. He wrote some notes in English and some in Latin, for scientists in his time often used Latin. Sometimes he scrawled in margins or over old writing, as if he were in a hurry or couldn't find spare paper right then. On the book's cover, Halley wrote:

> Edmond Halley, his Booke
> And he douth often in it Looke.

Each night, as Halley watched, the comet grew brighter. Each night, more and more ordinary people noticed it, even without telescopes. The comet became known throughout England as the Great Comet of 1682.

That August and September, as the new comet painted its bright tail across the sky, it was everybody's news. Ordinary people talked about it, and so did the scientists in the Royal Society at their meetings or in the coffeehouses where they sometimes gathered. Comets were a puzzle. The moon and the stars and the planets could be counted on. They were always there, where they were supposed to be. But comets were like flying firecrackers—here and gone, poof. Nobody knew what they were made of, where they came from, or where they went.

Scientists are not yet sure where or how comets form. Today, they believe comets are balls of dust and ice that are held in orbit by the sun's gravity. As a comet nears the sun, its ice warms and turns into a gas. The gas becomes visible as the comet's bright head and long, flowing tail. But for many ages, those who loved to watch the stars believed comets were accidents in the sky. They were exploded chunks of planets, or perhaps patches of air that had caught fire.

The glowing tails of comets make them seem to be blasting somewhere (even though comets move quite slowly, night by night). So people naturally thought of them as flaming cannon-balls or fiery rockets, and they felt afraid. Throughout the ages, people had believed comets brought warnings of bad things to come: famine, war, diseases. Many feared a comet might fall to earth and start a great fire. The comet would surely destroy the world!

Now, in 1682, people in the streets and shops and churches were again talking about the evils the comet would bring. They remembered the brilliant comet of 1664. The very next year, a terrible disease called the plague had killed thousands of Londoners. And the year after that, London nearly burned to the ground. Wasn't that proof that comets brought harm?

Sometimes, when Halley heard people tell such stories about comets, he must have changed the subject and talked about what he was actually observing, night after night. He was trying to find what kind of path the comet might be on, where it was going. As a scientist, Halley was interested in facts, not tales of horror and destruction from the past.

Astronomers already knew some facts about comets. They knew that comets did not come near the earth but were very far away—even farther than the moon. A Danish scientist named Tycho Brahe had proved this in 1577. They knew that comets travel in oddly curved arcs and sometimes speed up in their

comet's tail always points away
ese clues mean? Did they mean
in some sort of orbit around the
force?

oke and Christopher Wren had
. Wren had found a new way to
m the earth. And in 1678, Hooke
omet facts. He wrote that comets
sun. These paths, called *ellipses*,
es. Because the paths are closed,
n again and again.

tists also thought comets have el-
w. But none of them could prove
omers disagreed. A Frenchman
omets circle the sun. A German
travel a straight line, eventually
hought comets make an open arc,
and never come back.

theories, English theories. Circle,
. In London coffeehouses, Halley,
e broad, scarred tables and talked
of this idea and that. But no theory had been proved. No one knew what paths comets took and whether they returned.

Those autumn nights in 1682, when Halley would leave the cozy coffeehouses where people argued and guessed, the talk

Halley and other scientists often gathered in London coffeehouses.

of the evening filled his mind. Above the pitch-dark land, the comet's bright tail spread over nearly a third of the sky.

Scientific work often moves in stops and starts. It would be over twenty years before Halley published the prediction he is famous for today: that the Great Comet of 1682 would appear again in 1758. On those nights, he could only have had the faintest idea of this future.

Even today, when comets can be tracked by computers teamed with powerful telescopes, the job is tricky. But in Halley's time, the task was nearly impossible. Why tracking comets was so hard, and what it would take for Halley to do it, we shall see.

CHAPTER 2
HALLEY'S WORLD

O F ALL the English people who saw the Great Comet of 1682, few were more ready than Halley to ponder it.

Edmond Halley was born October 29 in either 1656 or 1657. He was the son of Edmond Halley, a London merchant, and his wife, Anne Robinson Halley. The older Halley dealt in soap and salt, and during Edmond's boyhood the family was prosperous.

The family name *Halley* rhymes with *alley*. It was also some-times pronounced "Hay-lee" or "Haw-lee," judging from other ways the name used to be spelled. Sometimes Halley spelled his first name "Edmond" and sometimes "Edmund." At that time, people often spelled their names several different ways, but he must have preferred "Edmond." He signed his will that way.

In 1665, when Halley was about nine, London suffered a devastating outbreak of the bubonic plague, a dreadful disease spread by fleas carried on infected rats. That summer, between seventy thousand and one hundred thousand people—one out of every four Londoners—died of the plague. Bodies lay in the streets, waiting to be carried off in carts and crowded into quickly dug graves. Anyone who could fled the city. The Halley family probably did, too, for they had a country house as well as a London home.

The next year, London nearly burned to the ground. Most houses and buildings were made of wood, and for five days flames ripped through the streets until four-fifths of the city lay in ashes. Over thirteen thousand homes and eighty-nine churches, some of them hundreds of years old, disappeared. Halley's father's business was destroyed and had to be rebuilt. For the young Edmond, it must have been terrible to see a huge city destroyed. First the plague, then the fire! London folk must have felt it was up to them to remake a whole world.

Other trials also struck the Halley family. Edmond's sister, Katherine, died in infancy, and a brother, Humphrey, died before reaching adulthood. And Edmond's mother died when he was only sixteen.

There are few records of Halley's youth. From sketches written later by friends, we know the young Edmond was slender, with brown hair. He showed inventiveness and leadership, liked people, and liked to talk. Friends described him as lively and witty. No one is sure what year he entered the famous London boys' school, St. Paul's. However, by 1671 he'd been chosen school captain, which was something like student president.

St. Paul's school was one of the best of its time. It had been founded about 150 years before Halley was born, during what we call the Renaissance (1450–1650). This was a time when people began to look at the world around them with a new desire to learn and explore. Cities sprang up where small villages had stood. Guided by the stars, ships sailed all over the world and returned with rare goods and new knowledge. After the printing press was invented in Germany, old knowledge could be translated and printed, and new knowledge spread.

Students at St. Paul's learned the languages of old books—Latin, Hebrew, and Greek—and also arithmetic, geometry, and trigonometry. And every boy studied navigation, the skill of guiding ships by the stars. Because England was becoming a sea power, navigation was thought to be an important skill for the future. Children studied it, just as today they learn to operate computers. Halley came to know the stars so well that it was later said if any one of them should shift, he would spot it.

Halley's father felt a good university education would help Edmond succeed in life, and he always encouraged his studies. He even had a special telescope made for his son in 1672, the year before he went to Oxford University. It was twenty-four feet long, and Halley used it for many years. Of this time he later wrote, "When . . . I first devoted myself wholly to astronomy, I derived so much pleasure and delight from its study as anyone inexperienced therein could scarcely believe."

The explorations of the Renaissance, on the earth and in the skies, made people see the world in a new way. For centuries, scientists and artists had pictured the earth as the unmoving center of the universe, under the dome of the heavens. They thought that a dome rotated around the earth, holding the stars. Inside this dome, other domes held the sun, moon, and planets in their places.

But now there were new ideas and a new method. Using the *scientific method*, which slowly developed in the 1500s, scientists observed occurrences in nature, formed a theory to explain them,

Old artists and astronomers thought the earth stood still under a dome studded with stars.

and made experiments to test the theory. They reported results other scientists could check and repeat. Important discoveries by men like Copernicus, Galileo, and Kepler showed the universe was not as the ancient writers had said.

In 1543, the Polish astronomer Copernicus wrote a book called *Of the Revolutions of the Heavenly Spheres*. He said the earth is not still but is moving! It turns on its axis, causing night and day, and it orbits the sun, causing seasons and years. The sun, not the earth, said Copernicus, is in the center of the universe.

Sixty-five years later, in 1608–1609, the Dutch invented the telescope. This made it possible to see the stars through magnifying lenses. Soon Galileo, an Italian, was improving the instrument. Now the sky seemed to open outward. Many new stars appeared, farther than anyone had seen before.

At the same time, Kepler, a German astronomer, discovered the planets, including Earth, moved in elliptical paths around the sun. With telescopes and mathematics, men uncovered new rules in nature.

Through the 1600s, men were experimenting with many different lengths and widths of telescopes. Some were shorter than your arm; others, such as the one used by the astronomer Hevelius in Poland, were up to 150 feet long!

Slowly, observers were discovering things every schoolchild knows today. People had known of six planets (as far as Saturn); by 1610 they had identified Jupiter's moons and by 1650 Saturn's rings. By 1673, the year Halley began his university studies, the French astronomer Cassini had determined the distance between Mars and Earth and established all the distances of the planets. He even made a good guess of the earth's distance from the sun. Other scientists found ways to measure the moon's distance from the earth and had studied eclipses.

Today, it is hard to imagine what a change in thinking this new picture required. No wonder people of Halley's time spoke of the "new science" or the "new astronomy"! If the new astronomers were right, stars scattered in all directions, perhaps to endless distances. If the earth was not the center of the universe, and if the universe was far larger than people could even imagine, what did that mean for man? These thoughts made people feel troubled and afraid.

At first, the new ideas of astronomy were like electric shocks in the world. Not everyone agreed with the new science. Even when Halley went to Oxford in 1673, some professors still thought the sun circled the earth! But by then the scientific methods of observation, experiment, and proof used by Copernicus, Galileo, and Kepler were accepted by most educated people.

King Charles II of England admired the new science and wanted his kingdom to outshine all others in discovery. In 1662, he chartered the Royal Society. In 1675, he asked Sir Christopher Wren to design an English observatory at Greenwich Park, near London. The main job of this observatory was to find a way to measure longitude at sea. Then ships could figure their distance east or west of home. Measuring longitude was a tough problem. It depended on exact timing of the moon's movement across the sky.

Science in England gradually became as popular as the king had wished. A wealthy Englishman might feel he should own a telescope with a fancy tooled leather or even sharkskin covering, gilt edging, and shining brass bands. And he should at least know which end of it a scientist looked through. Science was the fashion.

It was in this time of questioning and discovery that Halley grew up. He was only sixteen when he chose a career of studying the heavens. Astronomy seemed the most exciting work a young man could do.

CHAPTER 3
THE YOUNG ASTRONOMER

ONCE HALLEY had set his course for astronomy, it wasn't long before his work began to be known. When he was sixteen and still a student at St. Paul's, Halley wrote a remarkable letter to John Flamsteed, the royal astronomer. He politely corrected errors in some tables of the stars and moon.

In the style of that day, Halley's letter flattered Flamsteed. Halley also said his own telescope was exceptionally good and he'd be glad to be at the royal astronomer's service. It was his way of saying to the world he wanted to enter, "Here I am. Notice me."

And Flamsteed *was* impressed. He invited Halley to come to the Greenwich Observatory to use the fine instruments and books there. Halley and Flamsteed thus began a friendship that lasted several years.

In 1676, before he was twenty, Halley left his studies at Oxford with a daring plan. He wanted to chart the southern stars. The Polish astronomer Hevelius, the Danish astronomer Brahe,

Astronomers at the Royal Observatory in Greenwich.

and other men had made careful star charts for the Northern Hemisphere. But when ships sailed south of the equator, the sky was full of stars the sailors did not know. Ships could easily wander off course and lose their way.

Halley decided to travel to St. Helena, a tiny island south of the equator near Africa. There he would observe the southern skies. He hired a clerk (named Mr. Clerke) to accompany him and got permission from the East India Company to visit their trading outpost at St. Helena. For over three months, Halley and Clerke traveled by ship to St. Helena, carrying telescopes and other instruments.

It wasn't easy to watch stars from the small, mountainous island. Halley and Clerke had to lug the twenty-four-foot telescope, the five-and-a-half-foot steel-and-brass sextant (an instrument used to measure distance, in angles, between stars), and a bulky pendulum clock up a mountain to Halley's chosen spot for observing. During the first month, there was hardly a single clear night. The north wind blew cold and hard. Rain, fog, and mist rolled over the mountain. At night Halley and Clerke would catnap and wait for a break in the clouds.

In spite of continuing bad weather, Halley left a year and a half later with an amazing manuscript in his hand. It listed the positions of over 340 stars. He could use these lists to make new and accurate tables for ships' captains to follow. He had also observed and timed the passage of the planet Mercury across the sun.

On his return to England in 1678, Halley showed his work to several of the best-known astronomers, including Hooke and Flamsteed. All were astonished at what such a young man had done. Halley published a book titled *A Catalogue of the Southern*

Stars, and it was immediately recognized as very important to trade and navigation.

Flamsteed showed Halley's book to the king. Charles II was so pleased that he asked Oxford to award Halley his degree although he had not filled all the requirements. Soon Halley was elected the youngest fellow of the Royal Society.

Before he was twenty-two, before he ever thought of tracking comets, Edmond Halley, son of a soapmaker, had gained the praise of the Royal Society and the king.

That was only the beginning. The telescope had opened a doorway to space, and Halley worked on. In 1679, he journeyed to Hevelius's observatory in Danzig, Poland, to compare different kinds of telescope lenses and sights. (Hevelius had the largest observatory in the world. It sprawled over the flat rooftops of four buildings.)

Halley wasn't much impressed with Hevelius's 150-foot telescope. The supports kept sagging, and the telescope's sections couldn't be lined up! The slightest breeze made the whole thing wobble. And Hevelius used open sights on his sextants. English scientists thought these less accurate than sights fitted with lenses. Halley, too, preferred the English kind of telescopic sights. But he'd made a friend of Hevelius.

During the next two years, Halley traveled to France and Italy with a friend named Robert Nelson. Prosperous young English gentlemen of the day often rounded their education with a trip to these countries to see great works of art, but Halley's chief purpose was to meet other scientists.

In 1680, while riding a coach in the French countryside, Halley spotted a brilliant new comet. When he reached Paris, he observed it carefully. He heard France's leading astronomers talk of this new visitor. In January 1681, he wrote Hooke about the comet, asking him to "let me know what has been observed in England."

Soon he began sending letters to Flamsteed and Hevelius, requesting their observations of the 1680 comet. Meanwhile, with a busy pen, he tried to see if the comet's positions followed a straight path in space, as Kepler had thought. But he could not make his observations fit Kepler's theory.

In May he wrote Hooke that he was still trying to prove the straight-line path. He said, "It will be with a great deal of regret that I shall be forced to give over." But by the end of 1681, Halley *had* apparently given up, at least with this comet, at least for now. Halley saved his notes and traveled on.

Perhaps something about all this sky-watching led to romantic thoughts. While they were in Rome, Halley's friend Nelson fell in love and got married. Halley returned home alone, arriving in January 1682. Soon he, too, was alone no longer. That spring, he married a woman named Mary Tooke.

By all accounts, the Halleys were happy. But little is known of their personal life, for Halley never kept a diary, and his letters are almost all about scientific subjects. Of Mary we know only that her father was a bank official. The couple eventually had three children. Two daughters (not twins) were born in 1688. Their names were Katherine and Margaret. A son, Edmond, was born in 1698.

After their marriage, the Halleys settled in Islington, on the northern edge of London. In this house he set up his own observatory, equipped with his own instruments, including the twenty-four-foot telescope his father had given him.

That summer, secure and content, he began a series of careful, exact observations of the moon's path across the sky by night. This tedious project was aimed at solving the important problem of measuring longitude at sea.

Astronomy wasn't just a pastime for Edmond Halley. It was his work, and he loved it. His father, still helpful, gave him a generous allowance that the Halleys could live on while Edmond studied the sky. Halley knew he would spend his life doing what he could in this exciting science.

So it was not surprising that summer night in 1682, as Halley gazed at the moon and eased his telescope lens back and forth, that the light of the Great Comet should catch his eye. Comets. What paths did they follow, and how could the paths be traced? How did these puzzling visitors fit into the universe?

CHAPTER 4
THE PROBLEM OF COMETS

EVEN FOR a young, ambitious astronomer like Edmond Halley, tracking comets was nearly impossible in 1682.

It was no problem to record a comet's position among the stars. Halley's telescope and skills with a sextant were up to that. He could also tell exactly where a comet was in space by comparing its positions at different times. If a comet seen from London appeared one night between two stars in the handle of the Big Dipper and the next night appeared in the Dipper's bowl, Halley could look up the position of the Dipper stars on those dates, as they appeared from London. Then he could use geometry to find where that comet actually had been in space on those two nights. This step was called *reduction*. It meant adjusting the comet's positions, night by night, by subtracting the effect of the earth's own orbit. Kepler had done reduction to figure the planets' positions, and Halley understood how.

And the idea that comets had closed orbits and thus returned was in the air. Many astronomers thought that if the far-flung planets had elliptical orbits, then perhaps the mysterious comets did, too.

Then what was so impossible about the dream that slowly grew in Halley's mind?

First, comets don't follow the same rules as planets. Except when lost in the sun's glare, the planets are always visible. But comets come shooting out of who-knows-where, cross the plane of the earth's and the other planets' orbits, curve around the sun, and veer back off into space. A man's eye or telescope can see only the shortest wisp or curl of a comet's path. How could anyone tell for sure that a comet was following a certain trail?

Then there was the sheer number of comets cluttering up history. Bright, spectacular comets had spread across the English skies in a bewildering parade through the sixteenth and seventeenth centuries. Comets were easily seen, even without telescopes, in all of these years: 1607, 1618, 1652, 1661, 1664, 1665, 1672, 1680, 1682, 1683, 1684, 1686, and 1698! In the 1500s, likewise, fifteen large comets visible to the naked eye had been recorded. Which of all these comets would Halley begin to sort out, matching one path with another?

There was also the problem of math. Planets travel at nearly constant speeds in their orbits. But comets speed up and slow down, for they move faster as they near the sun. The math steps that calculate changes in the curves and speed of moving objects were not known to Halley.

Last, tracing comets was a waiting game. If someone predicted how planets move, there were the planets, right in the sky, waiting to be measured. A scientist could tell right away whether a guess was right. Planets were at least a bit obliging.

But comets were . . . gone. A scientist could have a theory about how they moved, and he could think the paths of two comets matched, but all he could do was *predict* a comet's return. He would not know if he was right or wrong. The answer would have to wait years—or centuries.

Yes, tracking comets was nearly impossible in 1682.

CHAPTER 5
HALLEY MEETS NEWTON

HALLEY'S FIRST MOVES toward the Great Comet in 1682 were nothing more than a set of exact measurements and some informal conversations with friends. That fall, only Robert Hooke read a paper about comets before the Royal Society. There was no paper from Halley. Not yet.

When Halley gave his next papers before the society, in 1683, they were on other subjects. And in the coming years, he would take up many other topics. In fact, for his work on a variety of tasks in the 1680s and 1690s, Edmond Halley slowly became the second most famous scientist in England. The best known was a man named Isaac Newton.

One of Halley's papers to the Royal Society in 1683 was about the variations of a compass needle. A compass needle does not always point exactly to the North Pole, or true north. In different parts of the earth, it wobbles and varies from true north. Halley wanted to see exactly how the needle varied. He hoped this would give more clues to the force of magnetism; perhaps a better understanding of magnetism might somehow help solve the problem of measuring longitude at sea.

Meanwhile, he carried on the moon observations begun in 1682 until the spring of 1684. Then personal troubles interrupted his work.

That spring, Halley's father was found dead in a river. No one knew just what had happened. Halley had to spend months working on his father's troubled financial affairs. Recently, the older Halley had had other problems, including an unhappy second marriage. Some friends believed he had killed himself, but a jury decided he had been murdered. To make matters worse, he left no will. The result was a lawsuit between Halley and his stepmother over Halley's inheritance. After June 16, 1684, there are no more records of Halley's moon observations.

When all was settled by 1685, Halley's income was less than it had been. To help him out, his friends in the Royal Society elected him their clerk in 1685. This meant losing a bit of pride. As clerk he had to sit at the end of the meeting table, and he could not appear in his wig. But the job paid a salary, and he liked his duties.

As clerk from 1685 to 1696, Halley kept records and answered letters for the Royal Society. This may not sound important, but letters to the Royal Society concerned all the important scientific discoveries of the day.

Halley's desk was like a huge seaport of ideas. He replied to scores of scientific inquiries and sent out scores of his own. What are you learning from your work with microscopes? he wrote to Anton van Leeuwenhoek in Holland. Did you succeed in making a furnace that burns its own smoke? he wrote a French scientist named Justel. He signed letters of recommendation for worthy inventions, like the following one for John Marshall, a maker of microscope, telescope, and eyeglass lenses:

I Have (by Order of the Royal Society) seen and examined the method used by Mr JOHN MAR-SHALL, for grinding Glasses; and find that he performs the said Work with greater Ease and Certainty than hitherto has been practised; by means of an Invention which I take to be his own, and New; and whereby he is enabled to make a great number of Optick-Glasses at one time, and all exactly alike; which having reported to the Royal Society, they were pleased to approve thereof, as an Invention of great use; and highly to deserve Encouragement.

Lond. Jan. 18. 1693, 4.

By the Command of the Royal Society;

EDM. HALLEY.

People sent him strange rocks and petrified animal forms gathered in faraway places and asked him to show these objects to the Royal Society. Halley must sometimes have wondered what would come next in his mail.

Halley also edited the society's journal, the *Philosophical Transactions*, from 1685 until 1693. It was the most important English scientific journal of those years. As both clerk and editor, he tried to settle quarrels between scientists and soothe jealousy and angry tempers. Halley had a gift for friendship, and he put his gift into the service of English science.

His jobs as Royal Society clerk and editor didn't keep Halley from his own work. Far from it. The more ideas that crossed his desk, the more ideas Halley had for his own experiments. From 1686 to 1696, the Royal Society heard over one hundred fifty papers presented by Edmond Halley. They were on an amazing variety of subjects: tides, gravity, archeology, magnetism, storms, light, underwater exploration, weight, and pressure.

Throughout his life, Halley presented papers before the Royal Society.

All this work was very important, but during these years Halley did something even more important. The story is one of friendship, insight, and determination.

Kepler had proved by observation that planets move in elliptical paths, not circles, around the sun. But what force kept the planets in their paths? Halley was one of many scientists trying to solve the problem: they all knew it was an important key to the workings of the universe.

In a London coffeehouse called Jonathan's in the spring of 1684, Robert Hooke often bragged to Halley and Sir Christopher Wren. He said *he* could show mathematically why planets orbit the sun in ellipses, according to Kepler's laws. But Hooke never supplied the proof. Wren grew tired of Hooke's boasting. To settle the matter, he offered to give a valuable book to whoever gave him the proof first.

Months passed, and Hooke still gave no proof. Halley knew he himself couldn't solve the problem, but he thought of another Englishman who might be able to. This man was a member of the Royal Society, and everyone thought he was a genius. But he didn't like to mix with people, and he was never there when the society met. His name was Isaac Newton. Had Newton also worked on the law of the planets' orbits?

In August 1684, Halley decided to travel to Trinity College, Cambridge, to see the quiet genius himself. And so he did, riding a coach on the bumpy, fifty-mile trip.

When he reached Trinity College, Halley wasted no time. Though Newton barely knew him, Halley immediately asked him whether he, too, had considered what force produced the elliptical paths of planets. Newton replied he had already solved the problem.

Astonished, Halley asked what he meant.

"I have calculated it," Newton said, according to Halley's later report to friends.

Halley had never expected this simple reply! Newton had worked the problem out, put the solution away, and gone on to other questions. Now he couldn't find the papers in his drawers! It was just like the strange genius to solve one of the dark mysteries of mathematics in his day and then forget to mention it to anyone!

Halley spent the afternoon with Newton. He begged him to search more for his notes or else rework the problem. He assured Newton his work should be published and would be appreciated. Newton did not enjoy publishing his work because he hated criticism.

Halley's visit drove Newton back to his earlier studies. Newton did rework his proofs about the planets' paths, and as the weeks and months went by, his ideas grew and developed into a much broader, more important work.

By November 1684, he had sent Halley a series of lectures in Latin about the motions of the planets. The excited Halley encouraged Newton to keep on. The result was Newton's book, whose full Latin title means "Mathematical Principles of Natural Philosophy." It was published in three volumes in 1687. Scientists today call the book the *Principia* (prin-KIH-pee-uh).

As the book was being prepared, Halley persuaded the Royal Society to pay for its publication. But when the *Principia* was ready, the society found it was short of funds. Rather than see this problem discourage Newton, Halley paid for the publication himself.

Halley also edited Newton's book, word by Latin word, all

250,000 words. He checked every proof, number for number, and helped develop the section on comets. Without Edmond Halley's friendship, Newton might never have begun or finished the *Principia*. It might have taken mankind many more years to find out very important scientific facts.

Newton's book showed the workings of gravity: how it controls the paths of planets, the tides, the earth's rotation, and all motions in the skies. To develop his theories, Newton had used a new kind of math he had invented, called *calculus*.

The *Principia* was a giant step for science. It went well beyond the work of Copernicus, Kepler, or Galileo (though it built on all of these). It was one of the most important works of physical science ever published until Einstein's work in the twentieth century. And, of course, the credit went to an English scientist.

The new king, James II, was very pleased—though we can be certain he never read the *Principia*, and neither did most of his subjects. Newton himself advised his readers to skip the first two volumes unless they knew a lot of math.

To those who understood his book, Newton became the leader of scientific thought. But because they couldn't understand what he had proved, some professors doubted Newton and the new science.

For Halley, there was still another result. In the third volume of the *Principia*, Newton said that comets, like planets, were part of the sun's family. Their orbits were controlled by its gravity. Newton proposed that some comets return and some don't. Those that hurl fastest follow a *parabola*, or open arc (a shape like a satellite dish). They curve around the sun under the force of gravity but then escape into space and do not return. Others, with a little less speed, are held in long ellipses, or closed paths.

They never leave the sun's control and return again and again.

Newton also showed how an astronomer could draw a comet's approximate parabolic curve around the sun if he knew just three of the comet's positions. This curve would give a scientist a rough idea of the comet's path so he knew where in the sky to keep looking for it. Further observations would show whether the comet's path was really the open parabola or the closed ellipse.

A comet is only visible when it is near the sun. In this brief part of a comet's orbit, it is hard for an observer to tell whether the comet is following a parabola or an ellipse. Near the sun, the two curves look almost the same. Even today, it is difficult to observe a comet's outward path long enough to tell whether its curve will close or continue on open.

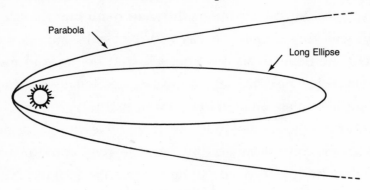

A parabola and long ellipse look similar as a comet rounds the sun.

But Newton had given Halley the missing tools he needed. Now Halley could map a comet's path. He could look for elliptical orbits—for comets that would come back.

Chapter 6
A Reasoner from Facts

A LTHOUGH NEWTON had shown the way, Halley's work
on comets would not move forward for several more years.
In the years following 1687, Halley and Newton continued to
share ideas, but both men were also at work on other tasks. The
1690s were an amazing time for English science, and Edmond
Halley was like a juggler standing in the center. His reputation
grew steadily as he put his hand on nearly every problem scientists were talking about. Often other scientists asked his advice
in solving problems.

One of these problems was how to measure things. Scientists
had just begun to accurately measure heat, pressure, weight,
time in seconds, and the flow of water and air. Thermometers,
barometers, delicate scales, better clocks, and wind gauges were
all new instruments. Halley was interested in every kind of
mathematical measurement—on earth, under the sea, or in the
skies.

In 1692, a Royal Society member named John Houghton asked

his "very ingenious friend" Edmond Halley for some help. Houghton, who wrote and published a popular journal about agriculture and trade, came to Halley with a curious question. Nobody knew what size England and Wales were. Could Halley think of a way to measure the land area?

Houghton expected Halley to draw up a plan requiring surveyors to measure every acre in England. When the Royal Society had helped to draw up a large new map of England in 1681, the surveying had taken four years. Now Houghton imagined another enormous job, for the outlines of counties meandered this way and that. And England itself was a most irregularly shaped island. Measuring England was like measuring the area of a huge jigsaw-puzzle piece.

Instead, when Houghton returned, Halley handed his friend a piece of paper. On it was written the total acreage of all the land of England and Wales!

Houghton asked how on earth Halley had done this. Surely the task should have taken years.

"I used nice scales," Halley said, according to Houghton's account. (*Nice* meant "precise" in Halley's time.)

Halley had taken the large map of England made in 1681 and very carefully cut out the land of England and Wales from the ocean. Then he weighed the paper cutout. Next, he cut out a circle from the map with exactly two degrees on the prime meridian for its radius. (The prime meridian is an imaginary north-south line on the globe through Greenwich, England.) Halley knew two degrees of the meridian equaled 138 ⅔ miles.

Now, by using geometry, Halley could find the area of his circle in square miles. All that was left was to weigh the circle and compare its weight to that of the large cutout. He could then

Halley measured the area of England without ever leaving his study.

find how many square miles England contained. Halley had measured the whole land!

In 1693, at Houghton's request, Halley published area charts for each English county. Once again, Edmond Halley was heard of far and wide. Halley, they said. That genius!

Houghton said he often turned to Halley because he was "always very ready to advise or assist in any thing that may do his country service."

One of Halley's tasks for his country took him away from London for several years. From 1696 to 1698, through Newton's influence, Halley became deputy comptroller of the royal mint at Chester. (A mint is a place where a government prints or coins new money.) Newton directed the task from London. Their job was to supervise the calling in and melting down of old, damaged silver money and the coining of new supplies. Unless the job was done well, England could be short of money for several months. The job required honesty and good judgment. It took a lot of time, but even from Chester Halley continued to show interest in many problems.

What causes weather to change? What causes trade winds and great seasonal storms like monsoons? During the 1690s, Halley studied these questions, and he presented his findings to the Royal Society. He was the author of the first known meteorological charts, or weather maps. He worked on ways to keep ships protected from ice damage so they could stay at sea in winter.

How many stars are there in the universe? Is the universe infinite, or does it end somewhere? Halley published papers on these questions as well. Late in life, he found evidence that stars do move in relation to each other. Before that, astronomers had thought that all stars are unmoving in space.

Halley was interested in all kinds of motion and how it can be measured. He even wondered about the tiny motions of living creatures, and he determined how fast a bird's wing must move to keep the bird in flight.

He also tried to learn more about the motions of an explosion. When Christopher Wren started rebuilding St. Paul's Cathedral after the London fire, he had used charges of gunpowder to blast away the ruins. Finally the neighbors made him stop because of the noise and flying objects. Halley must have passed the cathedral often during the more than fifteen years of its restoration. Why, he wondered, do windows fly outward when an explosion blows up a building? He wrote papers trying to explain this fact.

In the 1690s, Halley returned to an old interest—exploration under the sea. In an attempt to raise lost ships and valuable cargoes, he designed a diving bell. It could take four men fifty or sixty feet under water.

When the bell was sunk, trapping air underneath, the men could stay submerged for about an hour and a half. A waterproof barrel full of fresh air was sent down to the bell. A tube from the bell brought air to the helmet of a man who walked around outside under the sea. Halley spent a great deal of time in the bell himself, delighted with his experiment and with the fishes "in whose company I found myself."

While submerged in his bell, Halley found that when he cut his finger, the blood appeared green. He also noticed that the light coming in from a window in the bell's top had a cherry-red tint, while the light from the sea floor was green. He reported these curious facts to his friend Newton, who included them in *Opticks*, a book about light he published in 1704.

It seems there was nothing in the world that couldn't spur Halley on to measurements, experiments, ideas about *why*.

All Halley's ideas are not accepted today. He decided the earth must be hollow and there might be living creatures at its center. He said the comet of 1680 had a period of 575 years, but it later turned out he had mixed up this comet with another one. And he thought he could find the age of the earth by measuring how quickly water evaporates from the oceans over centuries, leaving the oceans saltier and saltier.

Halley's plan to take ocean samples in different centuries would have taken hundreds of years to try, and it would not have worked. The saltiness of oceans is affected by many things besides evaporation. But today we measure the age of ancient materials with something called the Carbon-14 test. It works the same way as Halley's plan, by measuring a rate of change in certain substances over a very long time.

Halley also had some interesting notions about the great flood reported in the Bible. Working from measurements of English rainfall, he calculated that forty days of rain would not supply enough water to swallow the whole earth to the depth the Bible reported. Perhaps, he thought, the flood had another cause, for the Bible also reports an inrush of water from the ocean. In 1694, Halley told the Royal Society that a massive flood could have been caused by a magnetic shift that pulled ocean waters up on the land. A passing comet could have caused that shift, he said. Today we know a comet is not large and heavy enough to cause such a shift.

Some of Halley's "wrong" ideas were very logical in his day. His theories were always bold and original. He reasoned from observed facts, and he followed that reasoning wherever it led.

Halley expressed his role as a scientist this way: "All that we can hope to do is to leave behind us Observations that may be confided in, and to propose Hypotheses which later Ages may examine, amend, or confute." Edmond Halley understood that this is the way scientific knowledge grows.

CHAPTER 7
THE LONG SEARCH BEGINS

IF SOMEONE said "Edmond Halley" in England during the 1690s, educated people nodded, but they didn't think of comets. In 1695, however, the busy Halley turned back to the old question of comets.

No one is sure why he resumed work on the comets in earnest now, not later or a few years earlier. Over thirteen years had passed since he first studied the comets of 1680 and 1682. Eight years had passed since his work for Newton in the *Principia*.

The *Principia* had stated that comets, like planets, move under the force of gravity and that some comets return. And Newton had shown how to compute a comet's parabolic path from just three positions. Now Halley undertook what he called an "immense labor." He wanted to find which comets *did* return. He decided to search out every old comet sighting he could find in history to see if he could track and match these comets' paths.

His plan had several steps. The first was to gather comet reports. Of these, he could use only sightings where an observer had noted at least three comet positions among the stars.

Then he could begin the calculations that would tell him where each comet's orbit lay. If he could find an orbit that was elliptical, that would mean the comet *did* return.

Meanwhile, comet by comet, he could start to look for paths that matched.

Today, scientists know that over 650 different comets exist. No one knows how many of these were listed in books available to Halley. Some writers believe he sifted through more than two thousand sightings reported in old books and manuscripts, looking for comets described by three reliable positions in relation to the stars.

In 1695 and 1696, Halley sat in libraries, consulting comet digests and old manuscripts. In the summer he opened windows for air. In the winter he wore gloves, for libraries were not heated. In those days, scholars would cut the right index finger away from their gloves so they could stay warm and also turn the pages.

Whenever an ancient writer mentioned a comet, Halley's eyes must have swept the page. Had the old astronomer plotted three exact positions for the comet?

Sometimes a writer would spend paragraphs telling much about the comet: how bright it was, its size, whether its tail was shaped like a fan, a fiery sword, a spear, a club, a dagger, or a halo. The book or manuscript might tell what direction the comet traveled in, how many people saw it, how many weeks or months it was visible, what happened on earth before or afterward, what the king or bishop said about it . . .

But such writers often failed to say where the comet *was*! Since the ancients believed comets wandered, they did not always think to note exact locations.

Sometimes the details Halley wanted *were* there, in print or scrawled out in the handwriting of some observer who had died centuries before. If he found these details, Halley would work out the path of that comet. Was the curve closed? Did the path match that of any other comet?

Each comet he studied required long pages of calculations. Of course, there were no computers or adding machines to speed the work. The pile of paper beside him grew taller and taller. But he wasn't sure what he had proved, if anything. He wouldn't know until he was finished.

In the midst of this work on old comets, Halley also studied the comets of his lifetime, particularly those of 1664, 1680, and 1682. Like a huge crop being harvested, reports on these comets came from everywhere—from the Paris observatory he'd visited in 1680, from Hevelius in Poland, from German astronomers. Only the notes of John Flamsteed, England's royal astronomer, were missing. Flamsteed had once been his friend, but as Halley's accomplishments grew, the royal astronomer had come to dislike him.

Halley asked Newton for help. Since the publication of the *Principia*, every scientist in England showed Newton great respect. Please write to Flamsteed, Halley wrote Newton in September 1695, and get his notes on the comet of 1682. I know he won't deny them to you. Newton did write to Flamsteed, and he got the observations.

Twice in his letters to Newton that fall, Halley made a startling point about the comet of 1682. "I am more and more confirmed," he wrote Newton on September 28, 1695, "that we have seen that Comett now three times, since the Yeare 1531."

Late in October 1695, Halley wrote Newton he was sure the comet of 1682 followed an elliptical orbit. From his study at Cambridge, Newton went over pages of Halley's calculations.

Both men wanted to be absolutely certain the curve was not open, like a letter U, but a closed ellipse.

Yes, Newton wrote his friend at last, I can agree with you. You have proven to me that the comet of 1682 has an elliptical orbit!

Certain of the orbit's shape, Halley continued his search for comet reports from many sources. He computed, checked, and recomputed paths. As he worked on each comet, he used several clues for its orbit. These clues were the basis for matching comets.

The first clue was direction. The Great Comet of 1682 had moved around the sun in a *retrograde* path, or backward from the direction in which planets and most comets orbit the sun. The comets of 1531 and 1607 stood out in Halley's lists, for they were also retrograde. The more comets he studied and checked, the more Halley realized how odd a retrograde comet was!

A second clue was the angle at which the comet approached the sun. This means how sharply a comet slants as it shoots through the plane of the orbits of Earth and the other planets, curves around the sun, and veers off again. That slant is called the *inclination to the ecliptic*, and no other astronomer had ever studied it before.

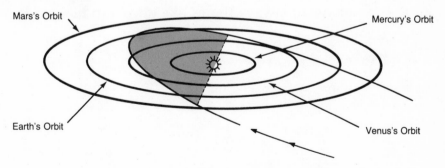

Inclination to the ecliptic of Halley's Comet.

Some other clues to a comet's orbit were the length of its long, looping path in space and the points where the comet came nearest to the sun and passed farthest away.

Halley's work that fall shows he had glimpsed the truth known today: the comets of 1531, 1607, and 1682 were the same comet, coming back. The comet's return must take seventy-six years, a little more or less. That was its *period*, or the time it took for one trip in its orbit. He told the Royal Society of his hunch in 1696, though he didn't publish a formal paper yet.

Having proven an elliptical path for the 1682 comet and suspecting "more and more" that the comets of 1531, 1607, and 1682 matched, Halley next did something surprising. He let the project drop! The last push, to final proof and publication, would not come for another ten years. Why?

One clue may lie in his next few letters. They show Halley ready to start work in the royal mint at Chester. His life took a left turn. In Chester, a small village with a great cathedral, he was separated from his scientist friends. He had sticky problems to solve—this time with the king's money. And the years ahead would also take him to sea.

So Halley waited. More earthly things again filled his days. But the comets were always there, like ghosts in his mind.

AN
ALLARM
TO
EUROPE:

By a Late Prodigious

COMET

ſeen *November* and *December*, 1680.

With a Predictive Diſcourſe. Together with ſome preceding and
ſome ſucceeding Cauſes of its ſad **Effects** to the *Eaſt* and
North Eaſtern parts of the World.

Namely, *ENGLAND, SCOTLAND, IRELAND, FRANCE, SPAIN,
HOLLAND, GERMANY, ITALY,* and many other places.

By *John Hill* Phyſitian and **Aſtrologer.**

The Form of the *COMET* with its Blaze or Stream **as it was ſeen** *December* the 24*th.*
Anno 1680. In the Evening.

Warnings of calamity after the appearance of the comet of 1680.

Old drawings of comets often showed their tails as flaming swords or daggers.

Halley's Comet in its 1910 appearance, its third return since Halley observed it.

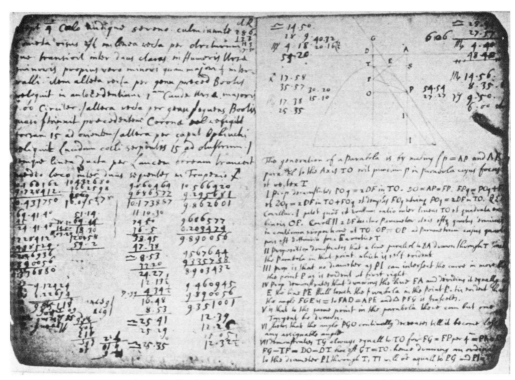

A page from Halley's first notes on the Great Comet of 1682.

Edmond Halley (1656?–1742).

Sir Isaac Newton (1642–1727)

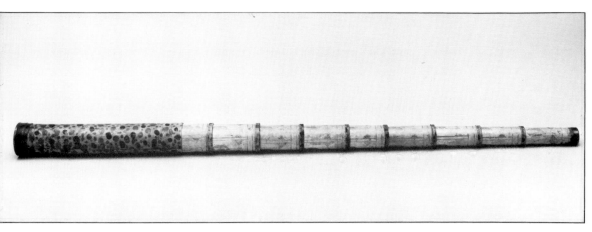

A long telescope of the kind Halley used. This telescope was made by John Marshall, a well-known maker of optical instruments.

Hevelius, the Polish astronomer, and his wife use a sextant with open sights.

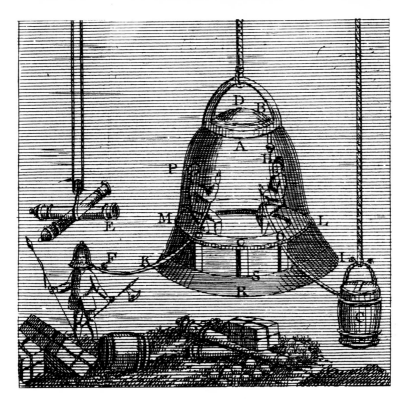

Halley's diving bell. "C" is the waterproof barrel of fresh air; "K" is the tube bringing fresh air to an explorer's helmet.

A reconstruction of Harrison's first sea clock (1730–1735).

When Halley's Comet returned in 1910, people still feared comets. This magazine drawing shows the tidal wave the comet might cause.

CHAPTER 8
CAPTAIN HALLEY GOES TO SEA

BY THE 1690s, the middle of his life, Edmond Halley was well known as a scientist of earth and sky. Now these busy years also found him going to sea, even to touch the shores of America. That adventure may well have started with a disappointment.

In 1691, Halley had been nominated for a professorship at Oxford. He wanted this job; it was an honor for anyone of learning. Many people, including scientists in the Royal Society, supported him. His chief critic was Flamsteed, the royal astronomer. Flamsteed went about saying that Halley had the wrong religious opinions and was of bad character.

At that time, it was necessary to have the "right" beliefs to get a job at an important university. Halley's letters say he was accused of believing the world is unending, which was not a belief of the English church.

Halley did not feel he held any unapproved religious opinions; in fact, in some of his scientific papers, he had stated that the world did have a beginning and end. He welcomed the chance to explain his views to a bishop. He was surprised when the Oxford professorship was given to another man.

Thus, in 1693, when a member of the Royal Society proposed an English scientific voyage around the world, Halley was interested right away. Perhaps he still felt stung at losing the Oxford professorship. Perhaps he was restless at thirty-seven. Or perhaps his wish to serve the nation's needs spurred him on. Halley began telling his friends he wanted to go on this trip.

During the next few years, the British navy built a ship especially for the voyage. Made in a Dutch style called a *pink*, the ship was named the *Paramour Pink*. Halley was appointed commander of the project in 1696, but it was not until he had finished his work at the mint in 1698 that he was free to go.

In October 1698, Halley received his instructions from the British navy. He was to observe the variations in the compass needle all over the Atlantic, find the latitude and longitude of all the places he visited, and discover whatever land lay south of the Atlantic! Captain Halley was not discouraged by the large order, and he set sail.

Before he had commanded the pink for a week, Halley found that the ship leaked and tipped to one side. Back he sailed to a harbor in the English Channel for repairs.

The *Paramour Pink* may sound like a cheery name for a wide-beamed, three-masted ship. But when he set sail once more, Halley found the men far from cheerful. His crew of twenty were tough sailors, and they did not respect this scientist as their captain. The angriest man was Halley's lieutenant, a man named Harrison. Halley learned too late that Harrison had once sent the Royal Society a paper on longitude that Halley as clerk had not accepted!

The mood on board quickly became worse. Early in 1699, as the ship sailed near Bermuda, off the coast of South Carolina,

Harrison loudly told the crew that Halley didn't know enough to captain even a tiny boat in a harbor. And the sailors used their own judgment in setting the ship's course instead of following Captain Halley's instructions exactly.

Halley took firm control. He put Harrison under arrest in his cabin and headed back home. He left the disagreeable Harrison and the difficult crew in England and set out on his scientific voyage a third time, with new sailors.

As Halley sailed the *Paramour* south over Atlantic waters, he met storms, icebergs, and thick fogs. Without any companion ship, he traveled far from the safer belts near the equator. His journals show his scientist's interest in everything he saw: there are notes about jellyfish, porpoises, strange swanlike birds, weather changes, and, of course, the positions of the moon and stars. All the way, he kept careful data on how the compass needle varied from true north in different areas of the ocean.

Halley returned with good charts of the magnetic changes in compass needles. He gained further information about measuring longitude. In 1700, he published charts of what are now called *Halleyan lines*. These are map lines showing the patterns of compass variations for the whole Atlantic surface. Like his comet work, this project with magnetism shows Halley gathering enormous amounts of data and organizing it into patterns, making sense of it.

Halley's work at sea soon led to another project. Queen Anne asked him to chart the tidal currents in the English Channel, the body of water that lies between England and France. The channel is known for its strong winds and rough currents, and it is treacherous for ships. For five months in 1701, Halley sailed the channel in the *Paramour*. He rode out frequent gales and was forced back into harbor four times by weather. But he got what he was after. He made guides to the channel's dangerous currents and shallow areas; these showed other captains how to use the tides to find safety. The British navy gave Halley a special prize for this work.

Halley went on two more royal errands as captain. In 1702 and 1703, Queen Anne sent him to advise the German emperor, Leopold, how to protect his ports. The grateful Leopold sent the queen a flowery letter praising Halley and also gave Halley a huge diamond ring.

Now Halley's fortunes brought him back on dry land. In 1703, John Wallis, a professor of mathematics at Oxford, suddenly died. Soon Halley's critic Flamsteed wrote a friend: "Dr. Wallis is dead. Mr. Halley expects his place, who now talks, swears, and drinks like a sea-captain."

Flamsteed's ill opinions didn't prevail this time. Halley was given the job. In 1704, over twenty years after he first saw the Great Comet, Halley was appointed the Savilian Professor of Mathematics at Oxford University.

As Savilian professor, Halley occupied a fine home at New College Lane, Oxford, as well as a home he kept in London to be near the Royal Society. Soon Flamsteed's letters to friends complained that Halley wouldn't live at the college, as a professor should, but was seeking a post in the queen's court.

But Oxford didn't listen. The college even built Halley a small observatory on the roof of his Oxford home. Captain Halley was Professor Halley now.

CHAPTER 9
THE SEARCH IS OVER

IN THOSE DAYS, an important university professor gave only one lecture a week. At Cambridge, Professor Isaac Newton would give his "with or without an audience," often with his stockings hanging down and an absent-minded air. Halley's lectures were no doubt more practical and lively.

Now, like Newton, he had time. He had the university's blessing for whatever research he pleased.

Halley hadn't been a professor long before he returned to his comets. The year 1704 found him at his quiet desk. The time for the last, long push of checking and calculations had come, and Halley was ready.

In 1705, Halley finished the work begun in 1695. He had calculated the orbit of every single comet he had found described by three positions against the stars. In all of history, there were only twenty-four such comets. There was one from 1337, another from 1472, eight from the 1500s, and fourteen from the 1600s. He'd found hundreds of other comets mentioned in old books and manuscripts, but without the positions he needed. He had piles and piles of calculations and notes.

Halley had decided to publish a complete table describing all these comets. He wanted to show future astronomers how to approach the tricky comets. A good pool of organized comet facts would give scientists a basis for recognizing new visitors.

From his mountain of work, Halley prepared a table that was quite simple-looking. The table was so neat and orderly that it made tracking comets look easy. There, in six columns, Halley showed the clues (such as direction and inclination to the ecliptic) he had found for each comet's path. He meant to be thorough, and thorough he was. He was getting ready to make a great public prediction.

If his prediction came true, he knew it would prove what his friend Isaac Newton had written: comets are parts of the solar system and follow the laws of gravity and motion.

As he finished checking and confirming his last notes and numbers in 1705, Halley must have felt a bit light-headed. His "immense labor" was over. He had mastered the comet he'd seen in 1682 on that summer night in Islington. Its period of seventy-six years was long in human terms, but short among comets. (Other comets as bright as Halley's have periods of over two hundred years.) The comet would not come back in Halley's lifetime, for he was nearly fifty years old. But it would return in the lifetimes of people now living, who might remember his prediction.

Halley's numbers told an amazing story. They showed the comet followed a very long, elliptical path out into space, a path that carried it over three and a half billion miles from the sun. He knew Saturn's distance from the sun was about 887,000,000 miles. This comet hurled four times as far as Saturn, the farthest planet then known. The comet's ellipse was incredibly, magnificently, elegantly long. Its path proved the truth of Newton's theory that gravity was a powerful force affecting everything in the universe.

Neither Halley nor anyone else had ever proved an orbit that lasted seventy-six years. The moon took just twenty-eight days to orbit the earth. The earth took one year to orbit the sun. Even distant Saturn orbited the sun in only twenty-nine years. But Halley had solid mathematical evidence for his prediction.

Halley published his comet studies in 1705 in a book called *Synopsis of the Astronomy of Comets*. It was printed in Latin at Oxford and in English at London, and it also appeared that year in the Royal Society's journal, *Philosophical Transactions*. Halley's work and his prediction became known to the whole world.

Halley couldn't say exactly when, to the day, the comet would return. He knew the pull of Jupiter and Saturn on its path while it sped through space might slow it down days or weeks. But it would return near Christmas in: $1682 + 76 = ?$

"How does he know?" some doubting professors still asked. Although Halley was respected, the findings of the new astronomy were still not accepted by all educated people. As the years went by, it wasn't just Halley's reputation that was at stake. It was the methods of the new science. If the comet returned, it would prove that Newton's principles could be used to make predictions about the universe—precise, well-calculated predictions that came true.

CHAPTER 10
PROFESSOR HALLEY, ROYAL ASTRONOMER

THE YEARS after 1705, when Halley published the *Synopsis of the Astronomy of Comets*, brought him honor and further accomplishments. But Halley never got over his comet fever. Even after the *Synopsis* appeared, he kept combing the world for comet data. The second edition of Newton's *Principia*, which Halley helped publish in 1713, grew fat with new pages on comets, thanks to Halley. One long passage lists every single recorded observation Halley had found of the 1680 comet, whether from Venice, the East Indies, or the English colony of "Maryland, in the confines of Virginia."

Halley's math gifts also made him a pioneer in studies of mortality, or how long people live. He used birth and death records to figure out the average life spans for different groups of people. His tables told insurance companies how much to pay people who subscribed to a type of retirement fund. Up to that time, life and retirement insurance did not have a solid mathematical basis.

As a professor, Halley also translated math books from several languages. All through his career, like many scientists then, he could easily hop back and forth from English to Latin. (He had even penned a long Latin poem in praise of Newton to open the *Principia*.) In 1704, he began to translate several books of ancient Greek geometry into English. When he found one valuable Greek book only existed in an Arabic translation, he sat there and learned enough Arabic to translate the text into English.

His writing and figuring never ended. From 1713 to 1721, Halley again edited the *Transactions* of the Royal Society. Now he was society secretary, a great honor. The Royal Society had grown larger and more important than ever, and its journal was read by scientists all over England and Europe. It was even faithfully read by English subjects in the American wilderness at places like Harvard and Yale.

Halley's role in the Royal Society once again brought him into conflict with his old rival Flamsteed, the royal astronomer. Flamsteed was always tardy in reporting his moon observations to the Royal Society. This upset the members. King Charles had founded the Greenwich Observatory in order to share English knowledge, not keep it a secret. When Flamsteed at last sent part of his work, Halley and Newton together ordered it published without Flamsteed's approval. Where material was missing, Halley added observations from his own work. The book was published in 1712.

Flamsteed was furious. Within a few months, he was able to seize the remaining unsold copies of the book. He tore out the pages based on his work and burned the rest. Flamsteed felt a scientist always has the right to decide when his work is ready to publish.

John Flamsteed died in 1720, his work on observing the moon still incomplete. King George I needed a new royal astronomer, and he appointed Halley. This time, there were no objections that Halley held wrong religious opinions or was wayward in his habits. His one bitter critic was dead.

Halley and his wife, Mary, moved to Greenwich, which is near London. They took over the royal astronomer's house in Greenwich Park. When they arrived, Halley found the observatory bare. After Flamsteed's death, his family had taken every telescope and instrument with them. (This was only fair, since Flamsteed had paid for all his own instruments out of his modest salary.) Nevertheless, all the new royal astronomer had to work with at first were some nice windows. None of the kings or queens of England had ever seen fit to allow their royal astronomer money for royal instruments.

Halley used his talent for persuasion. He obtained a grant from the king to equip the observatory, and he spent the money wisely.

Halley was now ready to resume tracing the moon's swift path across the sky. He meant once more to attack the problem of longitude at sea, the main task of the Royal Observatory. Halley had begun this project on his own in 1682 and continued it until his father's sudden death in 1684. He felt the best approach was to make exact charts timing the moon's movements over Greenwich, England.

As seen from Earth against a backdrop of stars, the moon moves approximately its own width in one hour. Because it's so large and moves so fast, it makes a good timekeeper. Halley thought that ships' captains could watch for the moon to cover a certain star. When this happened, they'd use star patterns to figure the local time at sea. Then they'd look at a chart that told what time the moon covered the same star over Greenwich.

What time was it at sea when the moon covered this star? And what time was it in Greenwich? The difference between times would tell the captain the ship's longitude, or distance east or west of Greenwich.

This plan was ingenious and, eventually, it worked. All ships needed were very precise tables of the moon's moves over Greenwich, England, against the background of stars. But to make these tables was no easy task.

Each period of twenty-eight days, the moon's path shifts. One full moon lines up with a certain star. The next full moon is near a different star. It takes eighteen years for the full moon again to reach that first star.

Halley's new tables of the moon would have to be made steadily over eighteen years. Although he was already sixty-four and unlikely to finish such a bold project, Halley set to work.

In 1728, when he was eight years into his observations, a man named John Harrison visited the Greenwich Observatory. He had come to show Halley a plan for a new invention: a clock that would work aboard ship to keep perfect Greenwich time. Taking a "home" clock along on a ship had always been the best solution to the problem of longitude, and every astronomer knew it. With a clock set to Greenwich time aboard, captains could directly compare Greenwich time with the time at sea to find their longitude. But no such clock had existed. The pendulum clocks of the day were not accurate on swaying ships.

Halley had seen a lot of proposed inventions over the years. What he saw before him now was good—very good. This clock didn't need a large pendulum.

In old age, Halley came by boat to London to attend Royal Society meetings.

Halley helped Harrison borrow money to make a working model of the clock, which Harrison called a *marine chronometer*. When Harrison showed the model to the Royal Society, the members quickly saw its value.

Harrison's clock would eventually make all Halley's long years of moon observations obsolete, and Halley knew it. Science was taking another lurch forward. Another man might have felt sad. But Halley helped the younger scientist all he could. To Halley, the new chronometer was one more stroke of genius for English science.

Almost to his last days, Edmond Halley remained an active scientist. Each Thursday, he would hire a boatman to row him up the Thames River from Greenwich to London. There he would join younger men at the meetings of the Royal Society. Later, some of them would gather for dinner in nearby Dean's Court; the spot was known for decades afterwards as "Dr. Halley's Club." The meal always consisted of fish and pudding, for by then Halley had no teeth.

Halley died at Greenwich in 1742 at the age of eighty-six. He did indeed complete the lunar tables he had begun so long ago. They were used for the next eighty years, until the chronometer became common.

Mary Halley had died five years earlier, after a marriage of fifty-five years. Edmond, their son, had died in 1741, so only their daughters Katherine and Margaret remained. Halley's grave lies in a small, bramble-covered churchyard, but his original tombstone is kept as a memorial at Greenwich, in the observatory wall.

At his funeral, Halley's friends felt sorry he had not lived to see whether his great prediction was right. He had charted earth, sea, and sky. He had followed tides and winds, traced the compass needle's shifts, mapped hundreds of strange stars, helped solve the problem of longitude at sea, and furthered underwater exploration. He had served the Royal Society and befriended other scientists for over sixty years. But in his scientific work, the comets had been a lifelong theme. "If the comet appears," he'd written to his fellow scientists, "remember it was predicted by an Englishman."

Years came and went. In the universities and among astronomers, Halley's prediction was not forgotten.

And in the year 1758, the prediction came true. On Christmas night, a German farmer named Johann Georg Palitzch, using his own homemade, seven-foot telescope, first spotted the comet's return in exactly that part of the sky where Halley had predicted it would appear.

The blazing comet grew brighter and brighter. All that winter, it streaked across the sky with its long hairlike tail glowing behind it.

By this time, telescopes were great, powerful instruments. All over the world, ordinary people as well as professors owned them. In 1759, every stargazing store clerk, every child and schoolteacher, and every great and famous professor had to admit one thing: Edmond Halley had been right.

Even the remote, unruly comets follow gravity's laws. And those with elliptical orbits come back on schedule. Newton's doubters were silenced.

Ever since that time, the Great Comet of 1682 has been called Halley's Comet. Each time this comet swings past Earth on its seven-billion-mile trip, Earth will greet it not as a fiery warning but as an old friend.

Genius has been described as "the art of taking infinite pains." Edmond Halley knew that scientific discovery rarely flashes down from the sky. It rises from painstaking observations and calculations, often over a very long time. Halley's work probed the darkness of space not with vehicles or missiles, but with the power of man's mind. His life, his bold methods, and his long search show us even today what genius depends on and what discovery is.

Exercises

1. Johannes Kepler, a German astronomer and mathematician, showed that the paths of planets around the sun were not circles but ellipses (flattened circles). Scientists think most comets also have elliptical paths.

An ellipse can be a near-circle (like the planets' paths), a long loop (like most comets' paths), or in between. Circles differ in size, but all have the same shape. Ellipses come in all shapes and sizes. You can experiment with drawing different circles and ellipses by following these directions:

• To draw a circle, drive a nail into a board on which you can draw with chalk or a pencil. Tie a string to the nail; then tie the string around the pencil. Practice drawing with the pencil held straight up until you can draw a perfect circle.

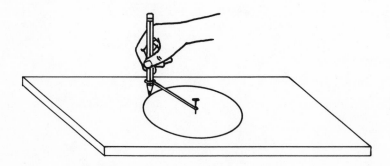

• If you lengthen the string, you get a bigger circle, but it's still exactly the same *shape*. If you shorten the string, the circle will be smaller.

• To make an ellipse, drive two nails into the board, about four to five inches apart. Take a piece of string twelve inches long and tie the ends together. Now loop the string around the two nails. Holding the pencil vertically, place its point anywhere inside the string loop. Push the pencil out as far as you can, and start drawing a line. Keep advancing the pencil around in a curving pattern, and you'll be drawing an ellipse.

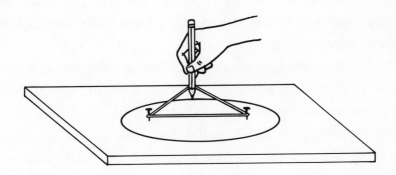

• Now shorten the string. How does the shape of the ellipse change? Next space the nails six to seven inches apart and lengthen the string to a fifteen-inch loop. How does the shape of the ellipse change? Remember that comets have elliptical paths of many different shapes.

2. You can have fun making circles, ellipses, and parabolas using a flashlight.

• Stand about two feet from a wall in a dark room. Hold your arm straight out in front of you and shine a flashlight on a wall. The beam will form a circle.

• Now tilt your arm up or down slightly. The beam will form

an ellipse (the path of a returning comet).

• Tilt your arm even further. The sides of the ellipse will spread out, and the beam will form a parabola (the path of a comet that never returns).

3. Men like Halley, who loved to watch the skies, gradually came to understand the paths of comets although they could see only a tiny portion of these paths. To understand why it was so difficult to figure out comets' paths, follow these steps:

• Let one person stand alone, representing the sun. Let another person, representing the earth, stand six or seven feet away. Earth orbits the sun in an ellipse. Let the earth person start to slowly orbit the sun person. Each orbit should last one minute, representing one year.

• Now a comet appears. From a door leading out of the room, let the person representing the comet dash in, run around the sun (passing through the space between the earth and the sun), and then disappear again, following a long, long ellipse. This trip (only a small part of the comet's total orbit) should take twenty seconds.

How could someone watching from the earth tell what path the comet was taking? The comet was only in view for a tiny part of its path.

4. For a long time, people believed comets were closer to the earth than the moon was. In 1577, a Danish astronomer named Tycho Brahe proved that comets must be much, much farther away than the moon. The following exercise explains how Brahe worked this problem out.

• On a blackboard or paper taped to the wall, write the numbers from one to ten horizontally, about one foot apart. Stand six to eight feet from the numbers. Hold a pencil vertically in your hand and stretch your arm out full length.

● Close your right eye and look at the pencil against the background of numbers. Notice which number it appears closest to. Now close your left eye and open your right eye. Look one-eyed at the pencil again. What number is it nearest to now?

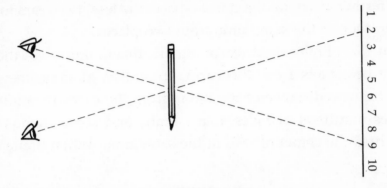

The background of everything we see in the sky is the pattern of stars. Imagine your pencil is the comet and your two eyes are two observers on earth. Just as your two eyes see the pencil in different places against the numbers, the two observers would see the comet in different places against the background of stars.

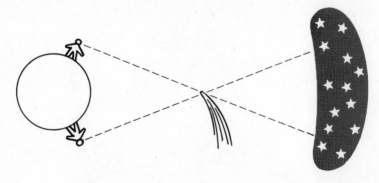

● Now hold the index finger of one hand about six inches in front of your nose and the other index finger at arm's length. Again, use the numbers on the wall as a background. Look at each finger, first with one eye, then with the other. You will find the farther finger appears to shift *less* against the numbers on the wall.

Imagine the stars are like the numbers on the wall. The moon is like your nearer finger, and the comet is like your farther finger. The farther away an object is in space, the less it appears to shift when seen at the same time from two places.

In 1577, Brahe used reasoning like this to figure out the distance of comets from the earth. (Scientists already knew the approximate distance of the moon from the earth.) Standing in places hundreds of miles apart, Brahe and some friends each observed the comet of 1577 at the same time. When Brahe com-

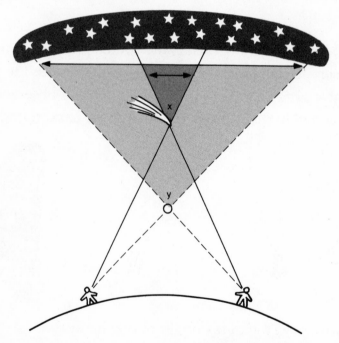

Angle x (the comet's shift) is smaller than angle y (the moon's shift). This means the comet must be farther than the moon.

pared the observations, he saw that the comet had barely shifted its position against the stars, while the moon had shifted position a lot. He concluded that the comet was very, very far away — much farther than the moon.

Brahe was using a kind of measurement called *parallax*, which means how far an object appears to move when seen from two different points against the same background.

Glossary

Astronomy: the science that deals with the study of the sun, moon, stars, planets, comets, and other heavenly bodies.

Axis: imaginary middle line around which a body spins. Earth's axis runs from its North Pole through the earth's center to the South Pole.

Calculus: an important branch of mathematics invented in Halley's lifetime by Isaac Newton and G. W. Leibniz. Calculus deals with problems involving the way things change. Using calculus, scientists can precisely determine how a hot object will cool or how a spaceship will move. A trip to the moon would have been impossible without calculus.

Chronometer: an instrument that measures time exactly. The marine chronometer invented during Halley's lifetime enabled ships' navigators to find their position at sea.

Comet: a heavenly body made of ice and dust, usually only a few miles wide. A comet is held in orbit by the sun's gravity. As the comet nears the sun, some of its ice heats up, turns into a gas, and boils away. The gas is what forms the comet's glowing head and tail.

Ellipse: a shape like a flattened or squashed circle.

Equator: an imaginary line around the middle of the earth half-way between the north and south poles.

Geometry: the mathematical study of points, lines, angles, plane figures (like circles, rectangles, and triangles) and solids (like cubes and spheres).

Gravity: the pull of one body on another. Earth's gravity makes things fall toward its center. The sun's gravity holds planets in their orbits. Isaac Newton described gravity as the force that holds planets, comets, the moon, and all other members of the solar system in their orbits.

Inclination to the ecliptic: the angle between the orbit of a planet or comet and that of the earth. (The ecliptic is the plane made by the earth's orbit.)

Latitude: distance north and south on the earth's surface, measured from the equator. On a map or globe, lines of latitude are drawn east and west around the earth.

Longitude: distance east and west on the earth's surface, measured from an imaginary line called the prime meridian. On a globe or map, lines of longitude are drawn on the earth from the North Pole to the South Pole.

Magnetic variation: the changes in the way a compass needle points away from true north due to the earth's magnetic characteristics.

Magnetism: the power to attract iron, steel, and some other materials. Electric currents, which result from the way atoms move around in substances, are the root of all magnetism, including the earth's. The earth's magnetism causes a compass needle to point north.

Navigation: the skill of guiding ships or planes. In Halley's time, navigation depended on knowledge of the stars. Today radio, radar, and other modern instruments tell a ship its position.

New science: the method of learning by observation and experiment which became widely accepted in the 1500s and 1600s.

Observation: a careful, objective record of an event or experience. An observation of a comet would tell exactly where it was in the sky, give the date and time, and describe its speed and direction.

Orbit: the path of one body around another which attracts it. The moon orbits the earth, and planets orbit the sun. Orbits are under the control of gravity.

Parabola: an open curve. Comets that move in parabolas instead of ellipses never come back.

Parallax: apparent movement of an object against a background when seen from two different observing points.

Period: the time it takes a body to make one trip in its orbit. Halley's Comet has a period of seventy-six years. The moon's period is twenty-eight days. Earth's period is one year.

Prime meridian: an imaginary line around the earth drawn through the north and south poles at Greenwich, England. The prime meridian is the starting line in measuring longitude.

Reduction: a mathematical step which removes the effects of the earth's motion from the movement of a planet or comet. Only by using reduction can scientists determine the object's true position in space.

Retrograde: motion around the sun opposite to that of the earth and the other planets. Halley's Comet has retrograde motion.

Scientific method: a way of studying nature by observing occurrences, forming a theory to explain them, and making experiments to test the theory. Using this method, scientists can report results other scientists can check and repeat.

Sextant: an instrument that measures the distance between objects in the sky in angles. A sextant is usually of metal or wood and has one moveable arm.

Sights: the part of a telescope, sextant, gun, or other instrument that helps the user aim straight or see a precise spot.

Telescope: an instrument invented in the 1600s that magnifies faraway objects with glass lenses or mirrors.

Trigonometry: the mathematical study of triangles; a branch of geometry.

Chronology

1656?   Born in London, England, to Edmond Halley and Anne Robinson Halley.

1671   While still a student at St. Paul's School, London, appointed school captain.

1673   Entered Queen's College, Oxford, equipped with a twenty-four-foot telescope his father had ordered made for him, along with other instruments.

1676–1678   At age nineteen, left Oxford with a clerk to sail to the island of St. Helena. There they observed stars from south of the equator.

1678   Published *A Catalog of the Southern Stars;* granted Oxford M.A. degree by order of King Charles II; elected a fellow of the Royal Society.

1679   Visited Hevelius in Danzig, Poland.

1680	Began study of comets; observed comet of 1680 from Paris; began tour of France and Italy.
1682	Married Mary Tooke and moved to Islington, where he had a small observatory.
1684	Visited Newton at Cambridge and learned he had worked out the math explaining the paths of the planets but had lost his calculations. Urged Newton to resume this important work.
1684–1687	Edited Newton's *Principia*. When Newton finished the book, Halley paid for its publication.
1685	Appointed clerk of the Royal Society.
1685–1693	Edited the *Philosophical Transactions* of the Royal Society.
1688	Two daughters, Katherine and Margaret, born.
1692	Designed diving bell and helmet; began series of underwater experiments.
1695	Began extensive mathematical work on the paths of comets; wrote Newton the comet of 1682 had also been sighted in 1531 and 1607.
1696–1698	Served as deputy comptroller of the royal mint, at Chester.
1698	A son, Edmond Halley, born.
1698–1700	Voyaged on Atlantic to study magnetism, winds, and problems of longitude and explore what land lay south of Atlantic.

1701	Charted tidal currents of English Channel.
1702–1703	Sent by Queen Anne to survey defense of German ports and harbors.
1704	Appointed professor of geometry at Oxford; resumed intensive study of comet paths.
1705	Published *Synopsis of the Astronomy of Comets*; it predicted the Comet of 1682 would return in 1758.
1713–1721	Secretary to the Royal Society; resumed editing its *Philosophical Transactions*.
1720	Succeeded John Flamsteed as royal astronomer.
1732–1733	Published last scientific papers, part of the eighteen-year project begun when he was sixty-four to follow a full cycle of the moon's positions.
1742	Edmond Halley died.
1758	Halley's Comet returned, on schedule!

Bibliography

Armitage, Angus. *Edmond Halley.* London: Nelson, 1966.

Asimov, Isaac. *How Did We Find Out About Comets?* New York: Walker, 1975.

Birch, Thomas. *The History of the Royal Society of London for the Improvement of Natural Knowledge.* London: Millar, 1756–1757.

Brandt, John, and Robert D. Chapman. *Introduction to Comets.* NASA/Goddard Space Flight Center. Cambridge: Cambridge University Press, 1981.

Branley, Frank. *Comets, Meteoroids and Asteroids.* New York: Crowell, 1974.

Branley, Frank. *Halley: Comet 1986.* New York: Lodestar, 1983.

Brown, Peter Lancaster. *Comets, Meteorites and Men.* London: Hale, 1973.

Calder, Nigel. *The Comet Is Coming!* New York: Viking, 1980.

Eddington, A.S., for the Astronomer Royal. "Halley's Observations on Halley's Comet, 1682." *Nature,* May 26, 1910.

Encyclopedia of Ships and Seafaring, ed. Peter Kemp. New York: Crown, 1980.

Halley, Edmond. *Correspondence and Papers of Edmond Halley*, ed. E. F. MacPike. Oxford: Oxford University Press, 1932.

Heckart, Barbara Hooper. *Edmond Halley*. Chicago: Children's Press, 1984.

Johnson, Francis R. *Astronomical Thought in Renaissance England: A Study of the English Scientific Writings from 1500 to 1645*. Baltimore: Johns Hopkins, 1937.

King, Henry C. *The History of the Telescope*. New York: Dover, 1955.

Land, Barbara. *The Telescope Makers*. New York: Crowell, 1968.

Ley, Willy. *Visitors from Afar: The Comets*. New York: McGraw-Hill, 1969.

Little, Bryan. *Sir Christopher Wren*. London: Hale, 1975.

Lyons, Sir Henry George. *The Royal Society, 1660–1940*. Cambridge: Cambridge University Press, 1944.

Moore, Patrick. *Comets: An Illustrated Introduction*. New York: Scribner's, 1973.

Richardson, Robert S. *The Star Lovers*. New York: Macmillan, 1967, pp. 77–80.

Ronan, Colin A. *Edmond Halley: Genius in Eclipse*. New York: Doubleday, 1969.

Sprat, Thomas. *History of the Royal Society*, ed. Jackson I. Cope and H. W. Jones. St. Louis: Washington University Press, 1958.

Stimson, Dorothy. *Scientists and Amateurs: The History of the Royal Society*. London: Sigma, 1949.

The author wishes to thank Sara Schechner Genuth, Assistant Curator, History of Astronomy Collection, the Adler Planetarium, and science writer Francis Reddy.

PICTURE CREDITS